The Thinking Tr

JEWISH FEASTS FESTIVALS, HOLIDAYS & CULTURE

Activity Book & Research Guide

Written by Sue Gerdes

Designed with Sarah Janisse Brown

Artwork by: Savannah Gerdes and Sergey Andreev

Introduction and editing by: Tony Gerdes

Contributions by: Melanie Potter & Ann Kofsky

www.annkofsky.com ~ JewishBoston.com

FUNSCHOOLING.COM

פסח

NAME:

DATE:

CONTACT INFORMATION:

SHEMA

שְׁמַע יִשְׂרָאֵל יְהוָה אֱלֹהֵינוּ יְהוָה אֶחָד

She-ma yisrael, adonai eloheinu, adonai echad

Hear O Israel, the Lord is our G-d, the Lord is One

בָּרוּךְ שֵׁם כְּבוֹד מַלְכוּתוֹ לְעוֹלָם וָעֶד

Baruch shem kavod malchuto l'olam va-ed

Blessed is the name of His glorious kingdom for ever and ever

וְאָהַבְתָּ אֵת יְהוָה אֱלֹהֶיךָ בְּכָל־לְבָבְךָ וּבְכָל־נַפְשְׁךָ וּבְכָל־מְאֹדֶךָ
וְהָיוּ הַדְּבָרִים הָאֵלֶּה אֲשֶׁר אָנֹכִי מְצַוְּךָ הַיּוֹם עַל־לְבָבֶךָ
וְשִׁנַּנְתָּם לְבָנֶיךָ וְדִבַּרְתָּ בָּם בְּשִׁבְתְּךָ בְּבֵיתֶךָ וּבְלֶכְתְּךָ בַדֶּרֶךְ וּבְשָׁכְבְּךָ
וּבְקוּמֶךָ
וּקְשַׁרְתָּם לְאוֹת עַל־יָדֶךָ וְהָיוּ לְטֹטָפֹת בֵּין עֵינֶיךָ
וּכְתַבְתָּם עַל־מְזֻזוֹת בֵּיתֶךָ וּבִשְׁעָרֶיךָ

You shall love the Lord your G-d with all your heart and with all your soul and with all your might. Take to heart these instructions with which I charge you this day. Impress them upon your children. Recite them when you stay at home and when you are away, when you lie down and when you get up. Bind them as a sign on your hand and let them serve as a symbol on your forehead, inscribe them on the doorposts of your house and on your gates.

To hear the Shema being recited, go to this link:

https://www.youtube.com/watch?v=vB58oyck-C8

TABLE OF CONTENTS

HOW TO USE THIS JOURNAL

This journal is a do-it-yourself research journal. We recommend using Jewish-authored books and websites to learn more about the holidays and celebrations mentioned in this journal. The following websites are full of valuable information and would be a good starting point:

www.myjewishlearning.com

www.chabad.org

www.aish.com

www.alephbeta.org

www.ou.org

There are also many wonderful books written about the Jewish holidays that will help you discover the rich history, culture, and meaning behind each celebration and guide you as you plan your own celebrations and traditions.

MY BOOKS ABOUT JEWISH HOLIDAYS & CULTURE:

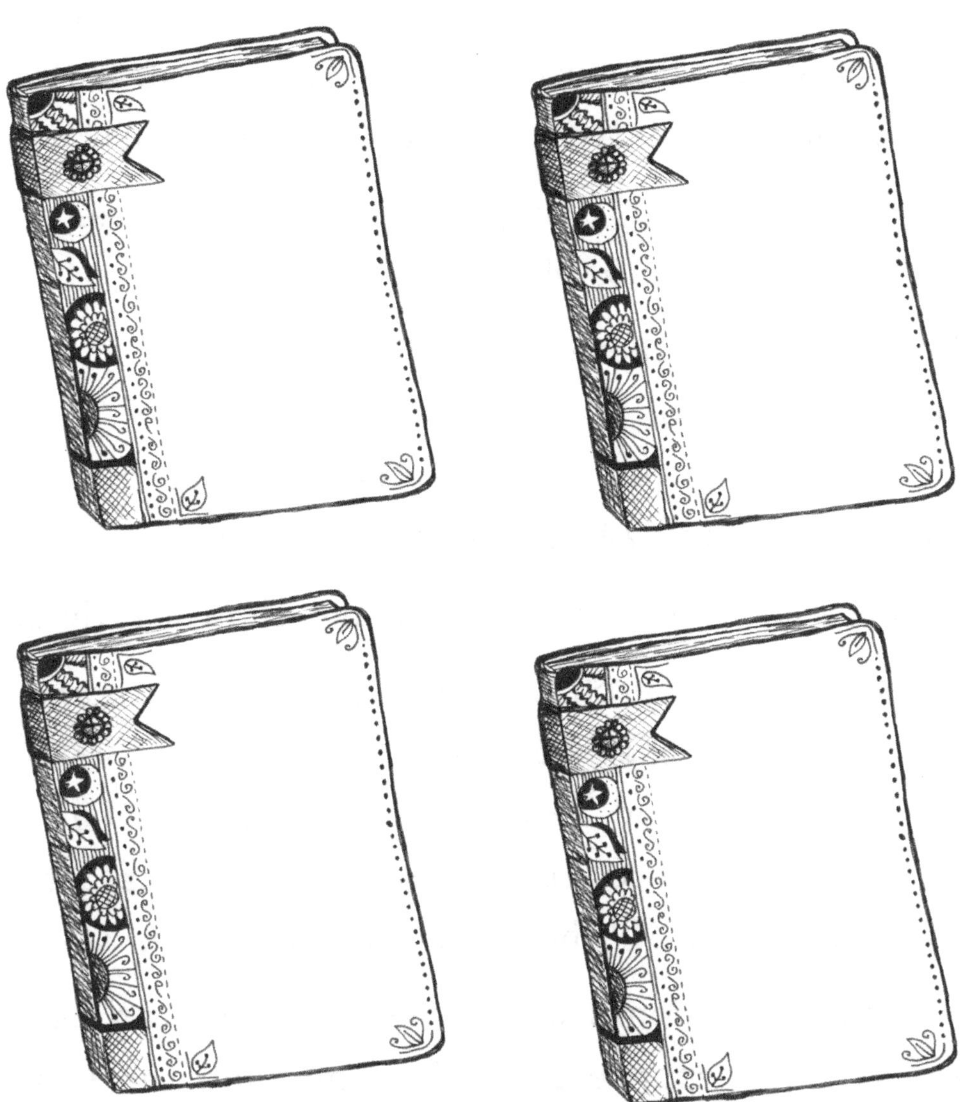

INTERNET RESOURCES:

INTRODUCTION

Jewish history and culture are remarkably complex. Some holidays are major and some are minor. Some holidays are ancient and some are modern. Some include feasting, some include fasting. As you start studying about the diverse Jewish holidays, it's important to understand something about the diversity of the Jewish people.

In over 4000 years of Jewish living, there has never been consensus on what a Jewish life should look like.

Census numbers vary, but there are approximately 14.7 million Jews in the world. About 6.7 million live in Israel and another 5.7 million live in the United States. The rest are scattered across Europe, Central and South America, Africa, Australia, and beyond.

For many, Jewishness is more like citizenship than a religion.

According to the Pew Research Center's *Jewish Americans in 2020* survey, 26% of Jews said they believe in the G-d of the Bible, 50% believe in a higher power, and 22% don't believe in either. The remaining 2% aren't sure. In contrast, over half of the general US population (56%) and 80% of Christians believe in the G-d of the Bible.

In addition, survey respondents were asked to name an essential part of being Jewish. The top response was "Remembering the Holocaust" at 76%. "Leading an ethical and moral life" was next at 72%. Even "Having a good sense of humor" (34%) ranked higher than "Eating traditional Jewish foods" (20%) and "Observing Jewish law" (15%).

Jewish religious beliefs, practices, and holiday observances vary greatly based on the movement (or denomination), though many Jews are not affiliated with any movement. So, if you were to ask, "Why do you light the candles for Chanukah?" you might hear, "Because G-d commanded us to light them" from one movement and "I think they look pretty" from another. Research Jewish movements to learn more.

If you're unfamiliar with Jewish holidays, you might find the traditions to be strange. As you study, be sure to use Jewish websites for your research. They will have an insight into the culture and Hebrew language that is important.

For example, in this book you will see "G-d." For Jews, the name of the Creator is the most holy word. Some have chosen to omit the "o" as a way of respecting the name by not allowing it to be destroyed or desecrated. Like much in Judaism, there is disagreement about this. For the sake of those who prefer "G-d," we will use that spelling.

The name of G-d in Hebrew is not uttered in synagogues, but Jews will say "HaShem" (the Name) or "Adonai" (my Lord) when referring to the Creator. Sage Abba Saul writes in the Mishnah that those who pronounce the name with its Hebrew letters will have no place in the world to come.

Adonai is plural to show G-d's greatness, since there are no capital letters in Hebrew. It's like using the "royal we" in English. Adon is singular and is used much more casually, like when Sarah calls Abraham her lord in Bereshit/Genesis 18:12.

When English bibles print LORD in capital letters, it is not a translation of Adonai. It is an attempt to copy the holy name of G-d, known as the tetragrammaton, the four Hebrew letters: Yud, Hey, Vav, Hey.

Sometimes English bibles will have "LORD G-d." This happens when the Hebrew uses the tetragrammaton and the name Elohim. Elohim is also plural and based on the Canaanite name El. This is why so many Jewish names contain "el" like Dani-el, Ezeki-el, El-ijiah, Micha-el, and so on. Superman's real name on Krypton is Kal-El, Hebrew for "voice of G-d."

Exploring a culture's holidays can be like visiting a new country without leaving home. As you discover the beauty and diversity of Jewish holidays, maybe you'll start some new traditions with your family. Shalom!

Scriptures:

SHABBAT

History:

Personal Thoughts, Prayers and Memories:

Planning:

Shopping List:

To Do List:

Customs & Traditions:

Recipe One:

Recipe Two:

Recipe Three:

Recipe Four:

MY FAVORITE CHALLAH RECIPE

Ingredients:

Directions:

Draw a picture or paste a photo of your challah here:

Prep Time:

Oven Temp:

Cook Time:

PRAYER FOR LIGHTING THE SHABBAT

בָּרוּךְ אַתָּה ה׳ אֱלֹהֵינוּ מֶלֶךְ הָעוֹלָם אַשֶׁר קִדְּשָׁנוּ בְּמִצְוֹתָיו וְצִוָּנוּ לְהַדְלִיק נֵר שֶׁל שַׁבָּת

Transliteration: *Baruch ata Adonai, Eloheinu Melech ha-olam, asher kidshanu b'mitzvotav vitzivanu l'hadlik ner shel Shabbat.*

English: Blessed are You, G-d, Ruler of the universe, who sanctified us with the commandment of lighting Shabbat candles.

Draw a picture or paste a photo of your Shabbat Candle Lighting here:

Copy the words of the prayer below:

____

____

____

____

THE 39 MELECHOT

In the Mishnah, there are 39 general types of activities that are prohibited on Shabbat. These 39 melechot are divided into 6 different categories based on the Torah reference from which they originate. Do some research and see if you can find the 39 melechot. Place each one in the correct category and then give a couple examples of each. The first one has been done for you.

Field Work (Numbers 1–11)	
1. Sowing/Planting (Zoraya)	
A. pruning trees	B.
2.	
3.	
4.	
5.	
6.	
7.	
8.	
9.	
10.	
11.	

Making Material Curtains (Numbers 12–24)	
1.	
A.	B.
2.	
3.	
4.	
5.	
6.	
7.	
8.	
9.	
10.	
11.	
12.	
13.	

Making Leather Curtains (Numbers 25-31)	
1.	
A.	B.
2.	
3.	
4.	
5.	
6.	
7.	

Making Beams of Mishkan (Numbers 32-33)	
1.	
A.	B.
2.	

Putting up/Taking down Mishkan (Numbers 34-35)	
1.	
A.	B.
2.	

The Mishkan's Final Touches (Numbers 36-39)	
1.	
A.	B.
2.	
3.	
4.	

MY SHABBAT MEAL PLAN

Observant Jews do not cook on Shabbat. Create a Shabbat meal plan that you can make ahead of time so that you do not have to cook on this day of rest.

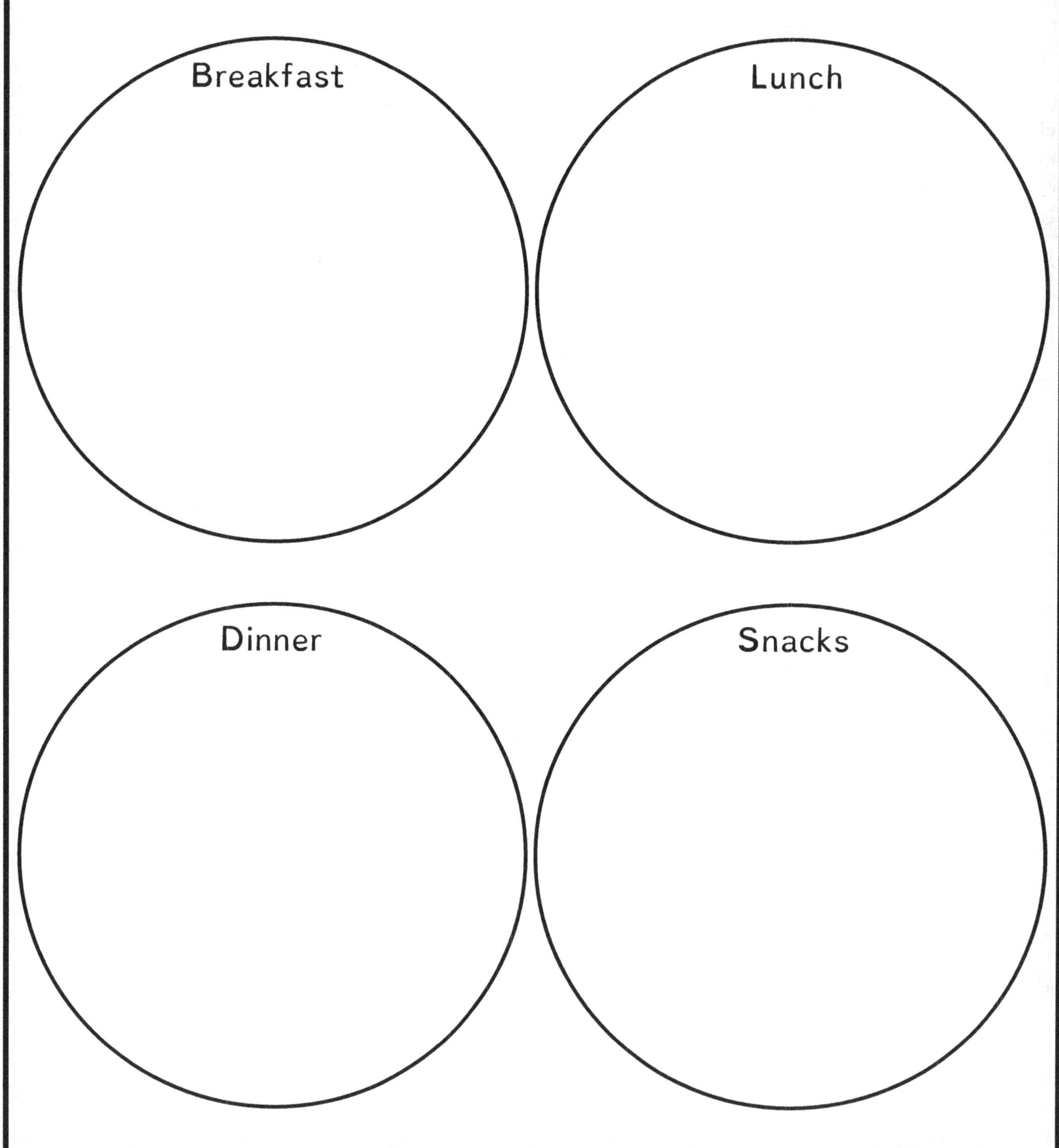

PREPARING FOR SHABBAT

Because the laws of Shabbat prohibit many household activities such as cooking, cleaning, using household appliances, doing laundry, shopping, etc., it is important to plan ahead so that you can enjoy your day of rest. Make a list of chores that you will need to do in each room of your house to prepare for Shabbat.

HAVDALAH: SAYING GOODBYE TO SHABBAT

The rabbis teach that on Shabbat, we are given an extra soul. At Havdalah we relinquish that extra soul, but hope that the sweetness and holiness of the day will remain with us during the week. We take a cup of wine, a box of spices and a beautiful braided Havdalah candle, and we sing or recite the blessings. (from *Havdalah: Taking Leave of Shabbat;* www.myjewishlearning.com/article/havdalah-taking-leave-of-shabbat/*)*

Visit the following link (or consult another book or website) to learn about how to make Havdalah: www.myjewishlearning.com/article/havdalah-taking-leave-of-shabbat/. Read the different prayers that are traditionally recited and copy them below:

Introductory prayer:

Blessing over the wine:

Blessing over the spices:

Blessing over the flames of the Havdalah candle:

Concluding blessing:

MY SHABBAT

Draw pictures, paste photographs, and journal about your

SCRAPBOOK

favorite memories of your celebration on these pages.

HEBREW VS. GREGORIAN CALENDAR

What are the major difference between the Hebrew and Gregorian calendars? Do some research and record your findings below:

The Hebrew calendar began on the first day of creation according to the Torah. Find out what Hebrew year we are in now:

When does the Jewish "day" begin and end? Why are Jewish days counted like this? How is this different from how a secular "day" is counted?

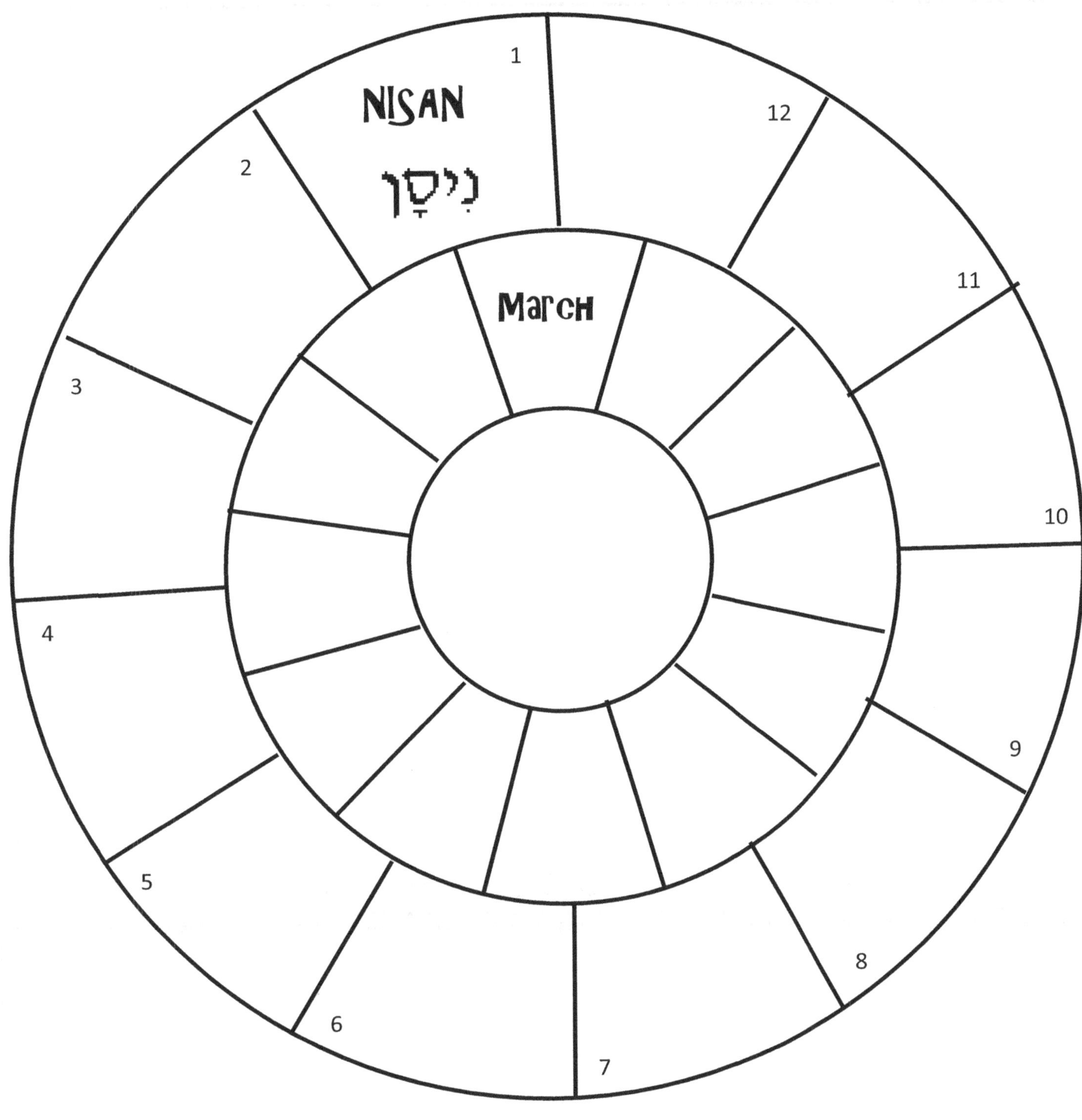

Instructions:

1. Write the names of the Hebrew calendar months in the outside circle going in a counter-clockwise direction (Hebrew writing is read from left to right). The first has been done for you.
2. Fill in the corresponding Gregorian calendar months in the inner circle going in a counter-clockwise direction. The first has been done for you. Hint: Each Gregorian calendar month is split between 2 Hebrew months.
3. Decorate your calendar wheel!

My illustration of Rosh Chodesh (The New Moon)

Scriptures:

ROSH CHODESH

Gregorian Calendar Date:

Hebrew Calendar Date:

History:

Customs and Traditions:

NISAN

Write 5 facts about the month of

Nisan

1.

2

3.

4.

5.

Scriptures:

PESACH (PASSOVER)

Gregorian Calendar Date:

Hebrew Calendar Date:

History:

Personal Thoughts, Prayers and Memories:

Planning:

Shopping List:

To Do List:

Customs & Traditions:

Recipe One:

Recipe Two:

Recipe Three:

Recipe Four:

THE SEDER PLATE

There are 6 elements of the traditional Pesach Seder plate and each symbolizes a specific part of the story of the exodus from Egypt. 2 other ingredients are also set on the traditional Seder table. Next to each item below, write down what it symbolizes. Keeping with the theme of Passover, what would YOU add to your seder plate? What would it symbolize?

1. Horseradish (Maror):

2. Shank Bone (Zeroa):

3. Fruit/Nut paste (Haroset):

4. Romaine lettuce (Hazeret):

5. Parsley (Karpas):

6. Hard-boiled egg (Beitzah):

7. Matzah:

8: Salt water:

9.

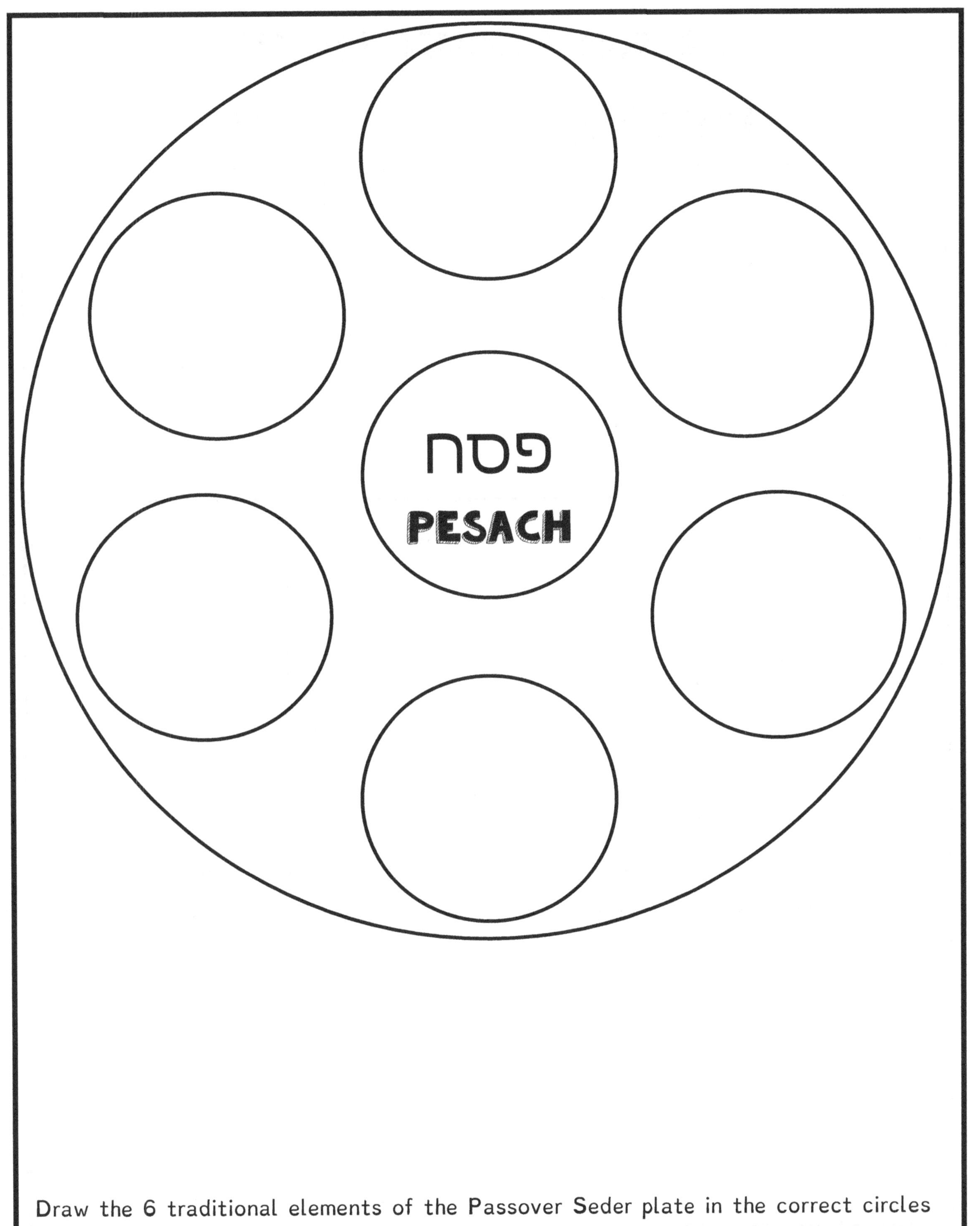

Draw the 6 traditional elements of the Passover Seder plate in the correct circles above. Add the 2 additional items and one of your own somewhere on the "table".

DESIGN A COMIC ABOUT THE STORY OF THE EXODUS

PASSOVER ORIGAMI FROGGIES

Follow these instructions to make bouncy origami froggies for Passover.
(Definitely more fun than the ones the Egyptians had to deal with!)

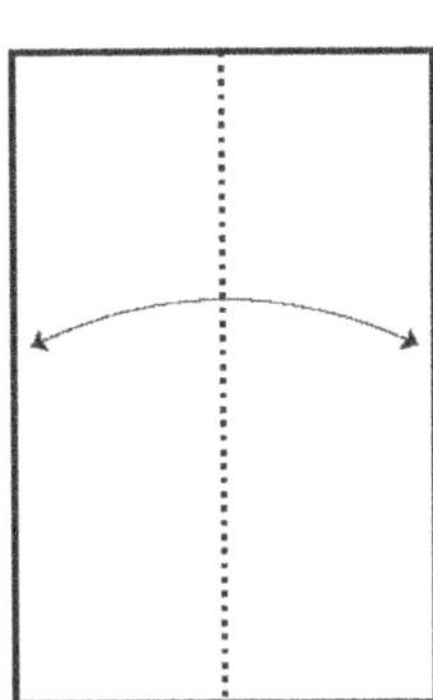

1. Start with a rectangular sheet of paper, white side up. Fold it in half, and open out again.

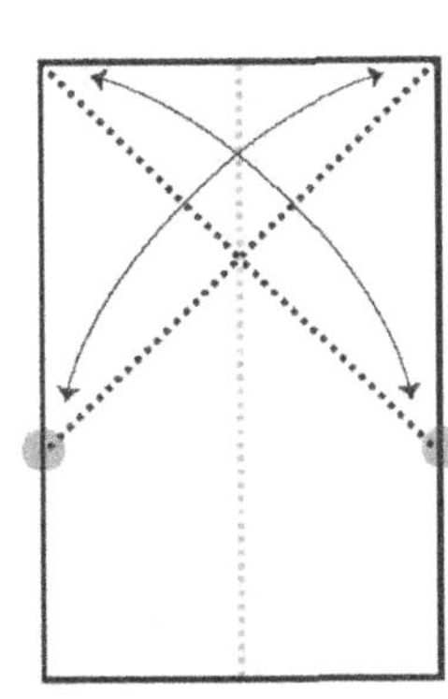

2. Fold both top corners to the opposite edge of the paper. Your creases should look like this.

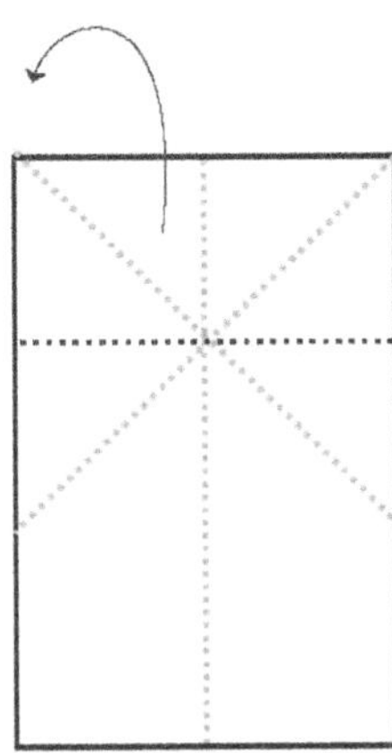

3. Where the diagonal creases meet in the middle, fold the paper backwards, crease well, and open.

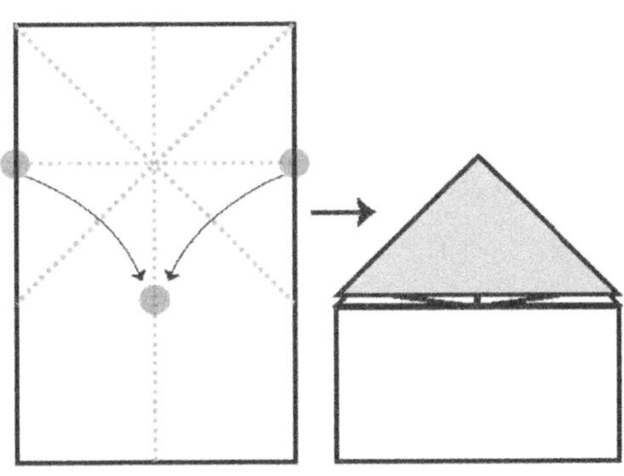

4. Holding the paper at the sides bring these points down to the center line, then flatten. The creases should do most of the work here!

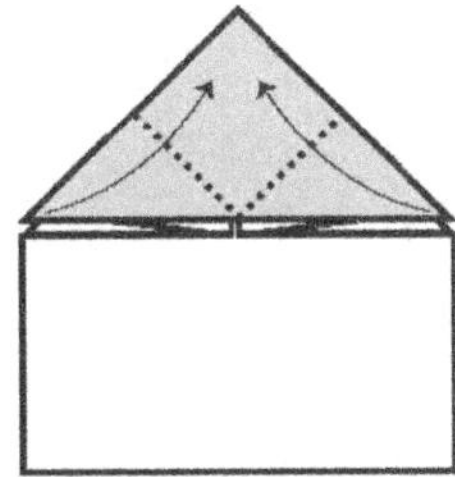

5. Fold the uppermost triangles up to the top point.

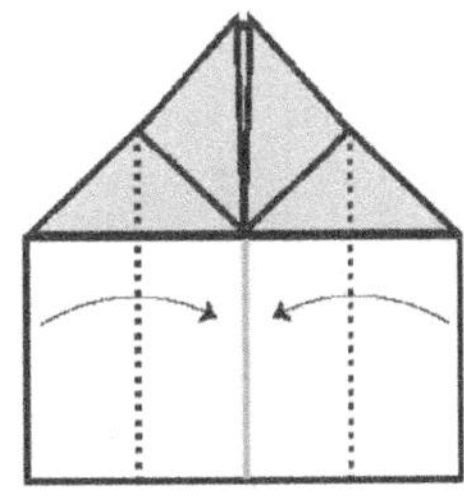

6. Fold sides in to meet the center crease.

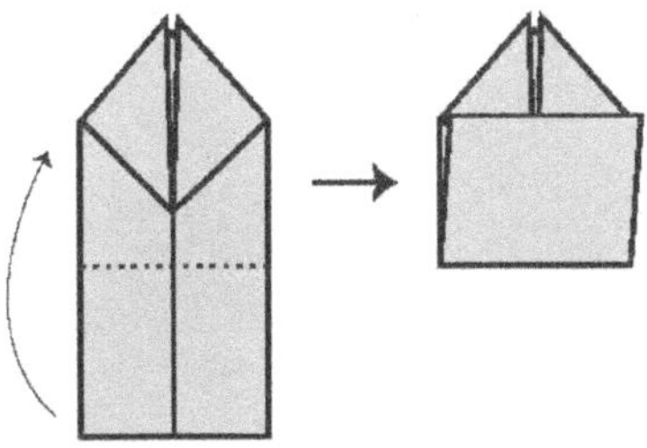

7. Fold the bottom of the paper upwards so that the end sits in the center of the top diamond.

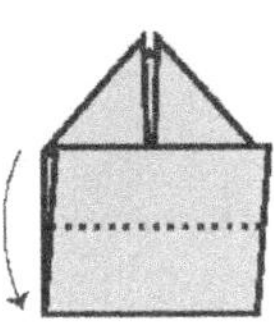

8. Now fold the same part downwards, in half.

9. Turn over, and your froggy is finished! Press down on his back, as shown, to make him jump. Boing boing!

Happy Passover from JewishBoston.com

MY PASSOVER

Draw pictures, paste photographs, and journal about your

SCRAPBOOK

favorite memories of your celebration on these pages.

COUNTING

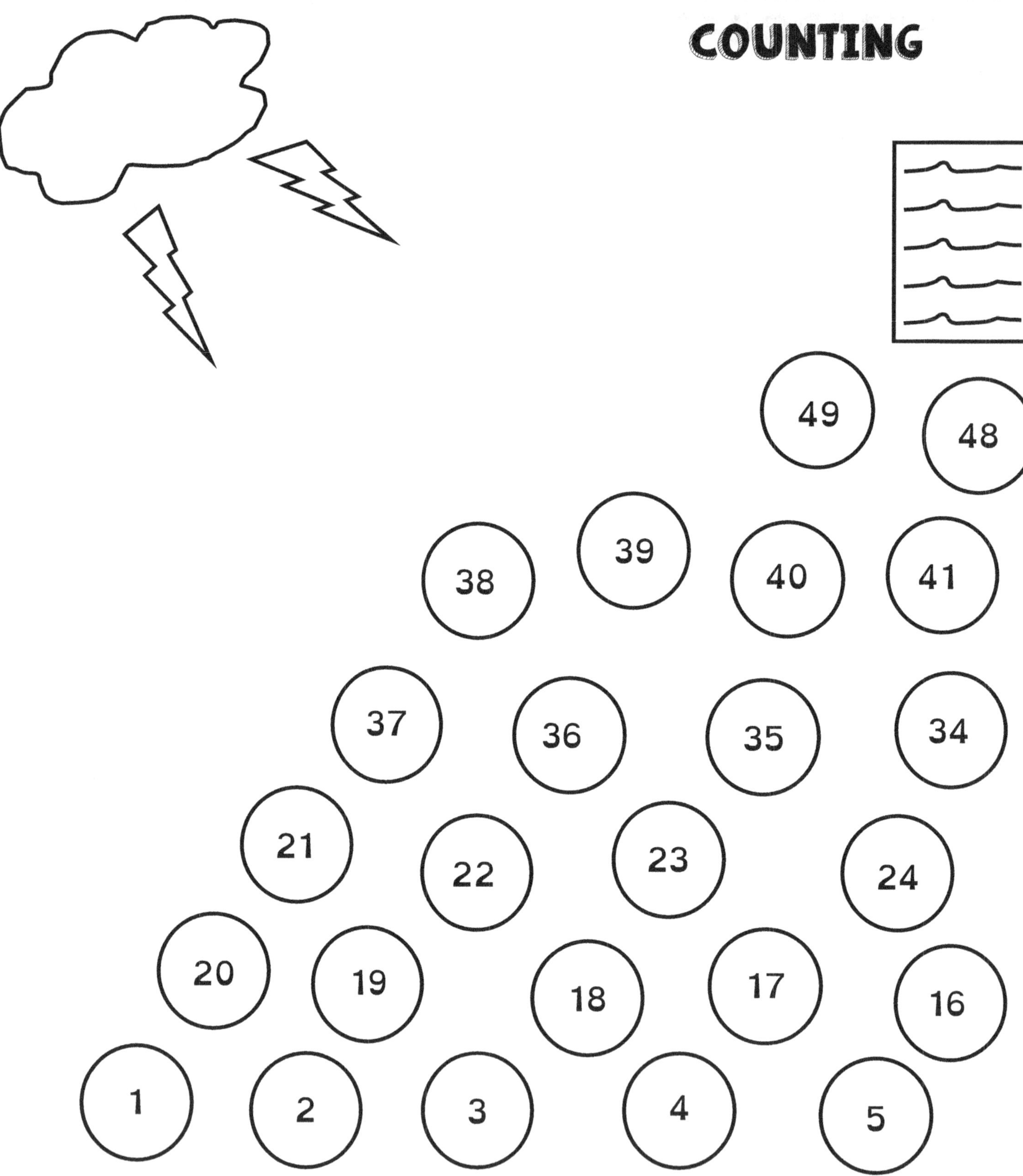

The omer (sheaf) is traditionally counted beginning on the 2nd night of Passover and continues for 49 days until the holiday of Shavuot on day 50. (See Leviticus 23:15-16) Each day, color in a numbered circle to count the omer!

THE OMER

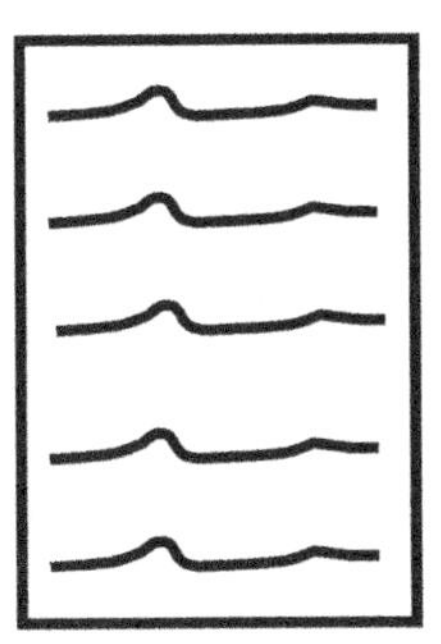

42 43 44

33 32 31 30

25 26 27 28 29

15 14 13 12 11

6 7 8 9 10

Scriptures:

YOM HA'SHOAH

Gregorian Calendar Date:

Hebrew Calendar Date:

History:

Personal Thoughts, Prayers and Memories:

Customs & Traditions:

Watch a documentary or YouTube video about the Holocaust.

Notes or Quotes:

____

____

____

____

____

____

____

____

____

____

____

Most Important Part:

Today's Date:

Choose a book about the **HOLOCAUST**. Write and draw about what you are reading.

READING TIME

Copy an interesting paragraph from your book or re-tell in your own words.

Illustration

WHAT WAS KRISTALLNACHT?

Research the event known as Kristallnacht. Pretend that you have been tasked with writing an article about this event for publication on *Wikipedia*. Gather your sources, take notes, and then write your article in the template provided on the next page. Don't forget to answer the 5 Ws: who, what, when, where, and why. Add photos or illustrations of this event. Make sure to list your references!

Notes:

Date:

Location:

Participants:

Outcome:

References:

THE "BYSTANDER EFFECT"

"All that is necessary for evil to succeed is that good men do nothing."
- Edmund Blake

1. What does this photo reveal about the behavior of non-Jewish neighbors during Kristallnacht?

On the morning of Kristallnacht, local residents watch as the synagogue is destroyed by fire. The local fire department prevented the fire from spreading to nearby homes, but did not try to limit the damage to the synagogue.

Ober Ramstadt, Germany November 10 ,1938.

- United States Holocaust Memorial Museum, courtesy of Trudy Isenberg

2. What responsibility does the bystander have in an event such as Kristallnacht?

3. Can you think of a contemporary event where the action or inaction of bystanders affected the outcome of the event? Explain.

BIOGRAPHY OF A HOLOCAUST SURVIVOR

Name:

Date/location of birth:

Date/location of death:

Photo

Significant life events:

1.

2.

3.

4.

Notable works, awards, accomplishments:

1.

2.

3.

Challenges this person faced:

1.

2.

What can we learn from this person?:

Interesting fact about this person:

MY YOM HA'SHOAH

Draw pictures, paste photographs, and journal about your

SCRAPBOOK

favorite memories of your celebration on these pages.

IYAR

Write 5 facts about the month of

IYAR

1. ____________________

____

____

____

2 ____________________

____

____

____

3. ____________________

____

____

____

4. ____________________

____

____

____

5. ____________________

____

____

Scriptures:

LAG B'OMER

Gregorian Calendar Date:

Hebrew Calendar Date:

History:

Personal Thoughts, Prayers and Memories:

Planning:

Shopping List:

To Do List:

Customs & Traditions:

Recipe One:

Recipe Two:

Recipe Three:

Recipe Four:

MY ACTS OF KINDNESS

There are many reasons why the Jewish people celebrate Lag B'Omer which falls on the 33rd day of the omer. Perhaps one of the most popular explanations can be found in the Talmud. The story goes something like this: During the season of counting the omer, which is a season of mourning, a plague killed thousands of students of the famous Jewish sage, Rabbi Akiva, because they were not treating each other with kindness. This plague ended on the 33rd day which could be one reason that Lag B'Omer became a happy day during this long season of mourning.

In remembrance of the thousands of students who were killed because they were not treating each other with kindness and respect, perform your own random acts of kindness and encouragement today. In each box, write or draw how you would encourage or demonstrate kindness towards someone today.

MY LAG B'OMER

Draw pictures, paste photographs, and journal about your

SCRAPBOOK

favorite memories of your celebration on these pages.

Scriptures:

YOM HA'ZIKARON

Gregorian Calendar Date:

Hebrew Calendar Date:

History:

Personal Thoughts, Prayers and Memories:

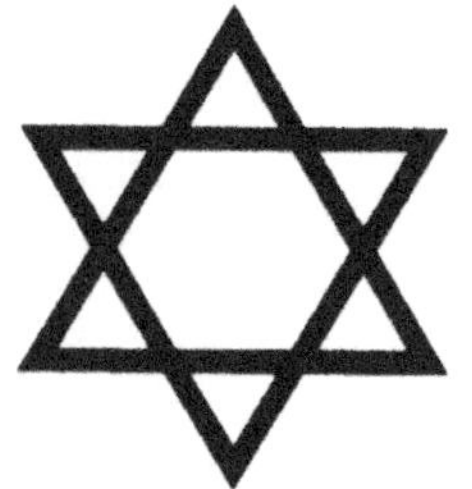

THE SILVER PLATTER

BY: NATAN ALTERMAN

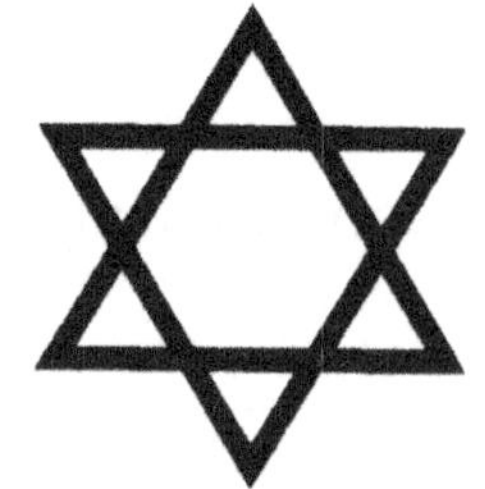

And the land grows still, the red eye of the sky slowly dimming over smoking frontiers.

As the nation arises, torn at heart but breathing, to receive its miracle, the only miracle.

As the ceremony draws near, it will rise, standing erect in the moonlight in terror and joy.

When across from it will step out a youth and a lass and slowly march toward the nation.

Dressed in battle gear, dirty, shoes heavy with grime, they ascend the path quietly.

To change garb, to wipe their brow, they have not yet found time. Still bone weary from days and from nights in the field.

Full of endless fatigue and unrested, yet the dew of their youth is still seen on their head.

Thus they stand at attention, giving no sign of life or death.

Then a nation in tears and amazement will ask, "Who are you?"

And they will answer quietly, "We are the silver platter on which the Jewish state was given."

Thus they will say and fall back in shadows. And the rest will be told in the chronicles of Israel.

Nathan Alterman wrote the poem, *The Silver Platter*, during the 1948 War of Independence. It used to be a common reading during Yom Ha'Zikaron ceremonies but after The Six Day War (1967) and the Yom Kippur War (1973), it was replaced with newer poems and songs.

Copy the words of the poem, "The Silver Platter"

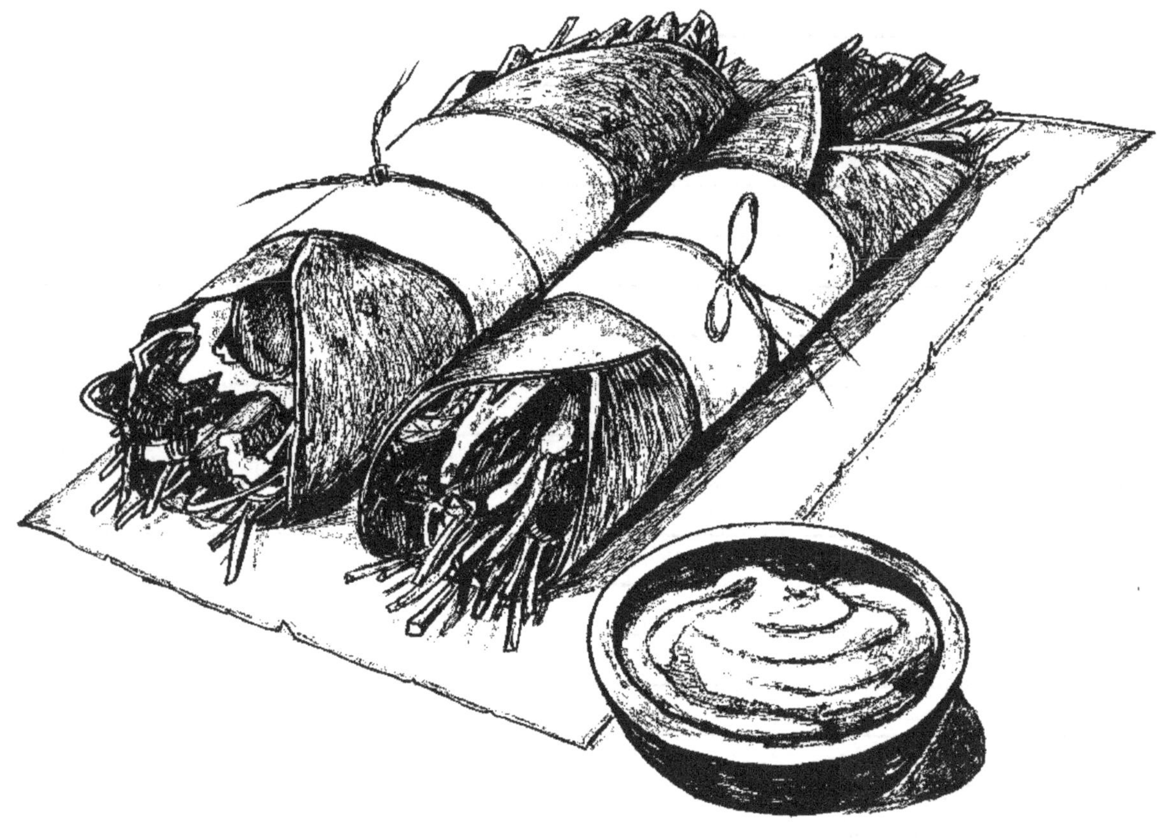

Scriptures:

YOM HA'ATZMAUT

Gregorian Calendar Date:

Hebrew Calendar Date:

History:

Personal Thoughts, Prayers and Memories:

Recipe One:

Recipe Two:

Recipe Three:

Recipe Four:

ISRAEL INDEPENDENCE DAY

Write 4 facts about Yom Ha'Atzmaut (Israel Independence Day):

1.

2.

3.

4.

Color the flag of Israel

MAKE YOM HA'ATZMAUT PINWHEELS

1. Decorate a 6 x 6 in. square piece of paper with colors & symbols of Israel.

2. Cut each corner up to about an inch away from the center. Poke a small hole in alternating corners of the square paper and the center of the paper (see diagram).

3. Bring the corners with the holes into the center (do not crease) and put a pipe cleaner through the center as shown.

4. Twist the pipe cleaner around the pencil in the front to form a "knot" that will keep the pinwheel on the pipe cleaner. Remove the pencil.

5. Staple the corners at the center.

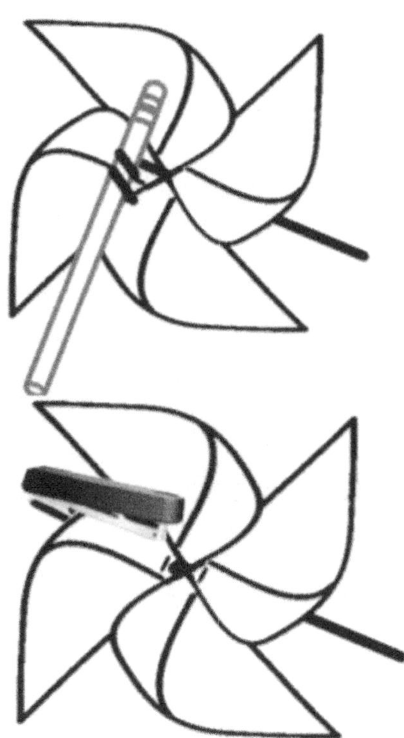

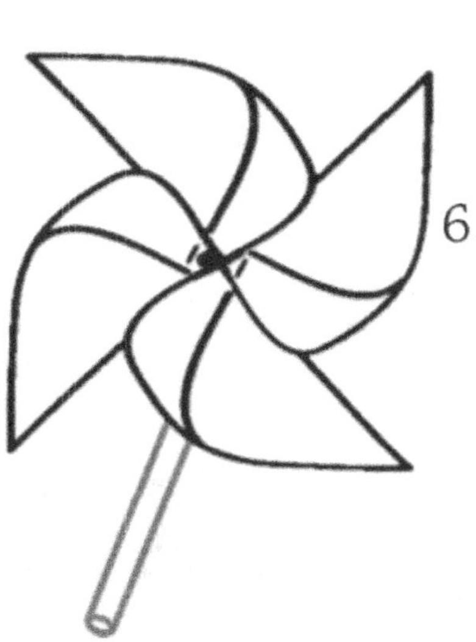

6. Secure the pipe cleaner to the pencil in the back.

"HATIKVAH" (ISRAEL'S NATIONAL ANTHEM)

Words by: Naphtali Herz Imber

English translation:	Hebrew transliteration:
As long as within our hearts	Kol od ba'le'vav p'nima,
The Jewish soul sings,	Nefesh yehudi ho'miyah.
As long as forward to the East	U'lefa-atei mizrach kadimah,
To Zion, looks the eye –	Ayin le'Tziyyon tzofiyah.
Our hope is not yet lost,	Od lo avda tikva-teinu,
It is two thousand years old,	Ha'tikvah bat sh'not al-payim
To be a free people in our land	Lih-yot am chofshi b'ar-tzeinu
The land of Zion and Jerusalem.	Eretz Tziyyon v'Yerushalayim.

To listen to "Hatikvah " being sung, visit this link:
https://www.youtube.com/watch?v=RHaopDM6fHw&feature=emb_logo

Copy the words of "Hatikvah", Israel's National Anthem, below:

Illustration

MY YOM HA'ATZMAUT

Draw pictures, paste photographs, and journal about your

SCRAPBOOK

favorite memories of your celebration on these pages.

SIVAN

Write 5 facts about the month of

SIVAN

1.

2

3.

4.

5.

Scriptures:

SHAVUOT

Gregorian Calendar Date:

Hebrew Calendar Date:

History:

Personal Thoughts, Prayers and Memories:

Planning:

Shopping List:

To Do List:

Customs & Traditions:

Recipe One:

Recipe Two:

Recipe Three:

Recipe Four:

THE GIVING

Shavuot is identified with the giving of the Torah on Mount Sinai. Write the 10 Commandments on the tablets:

OF THE TORAH

6.

7.

8.

9.

10.

THE BOOK OF RUTH

The book of Ruth is traditionally read on the second day of Shavuot. Scholars disagree on why this particular book is read. Do some research and write down 3 possible reasons why the book of Ruth is read on Shavuot:

1.

2.

3.

On the next page, create a comic to tell the story of Ruth.

MY SHAVUOT

Draw pictures, paste photographs, and journal about your

SCRAPBOOK

favorite memories of your celebration on these pages.

TAMMUZ

Write 5 facts about the month of

TAMMUZ

1.

2

3.

4.

5.

AV

Write 5 facts about the month of

AV

1.

2

3.

4.

5.

Scriptures:

TISHA B'AV

Gregorian Calendar Date:

Hebrew Calendar Date:

History:

Personal Thoughts, Prayers and Memories:

TISHA B'AV: A DAY OF MOURNING

The 9th day of the month of Av, Tisha B'Av, is a communal day of intense mourning among Jewish people around the world. Many tragic events are said to have occurred on this day in history, including the two for which this day is traditionally observed. Do some research and write down 6 of these events:

1. ______________________________

2 ______________________________

3 ______________________________

4 ______________________________

5 ______________________________

6 ______________________________

Customs & Traditions:

Scriptures:

TU B'AV

Gregorian Calendar Date:

Hebrew Calendar Date:

History:

Personal Thoughts, Prayers and Memories:

Planning:

Shopping List:

To Do List:

Customs & Traditions:

Recipe One:

Recipe Two:

Recipe Three:

Recipe Four:

TU B'AV: THE JEWISH DAY OF LOVE

5 ways that I can show love today:

MY FAVORITE TU B'AV COOKIE RECIPE

Ingredients:

Directions:

Draw a picture or paste a photo of your cookies here

Prep Time:

Oven Temp:

Cook Time:

ELUL

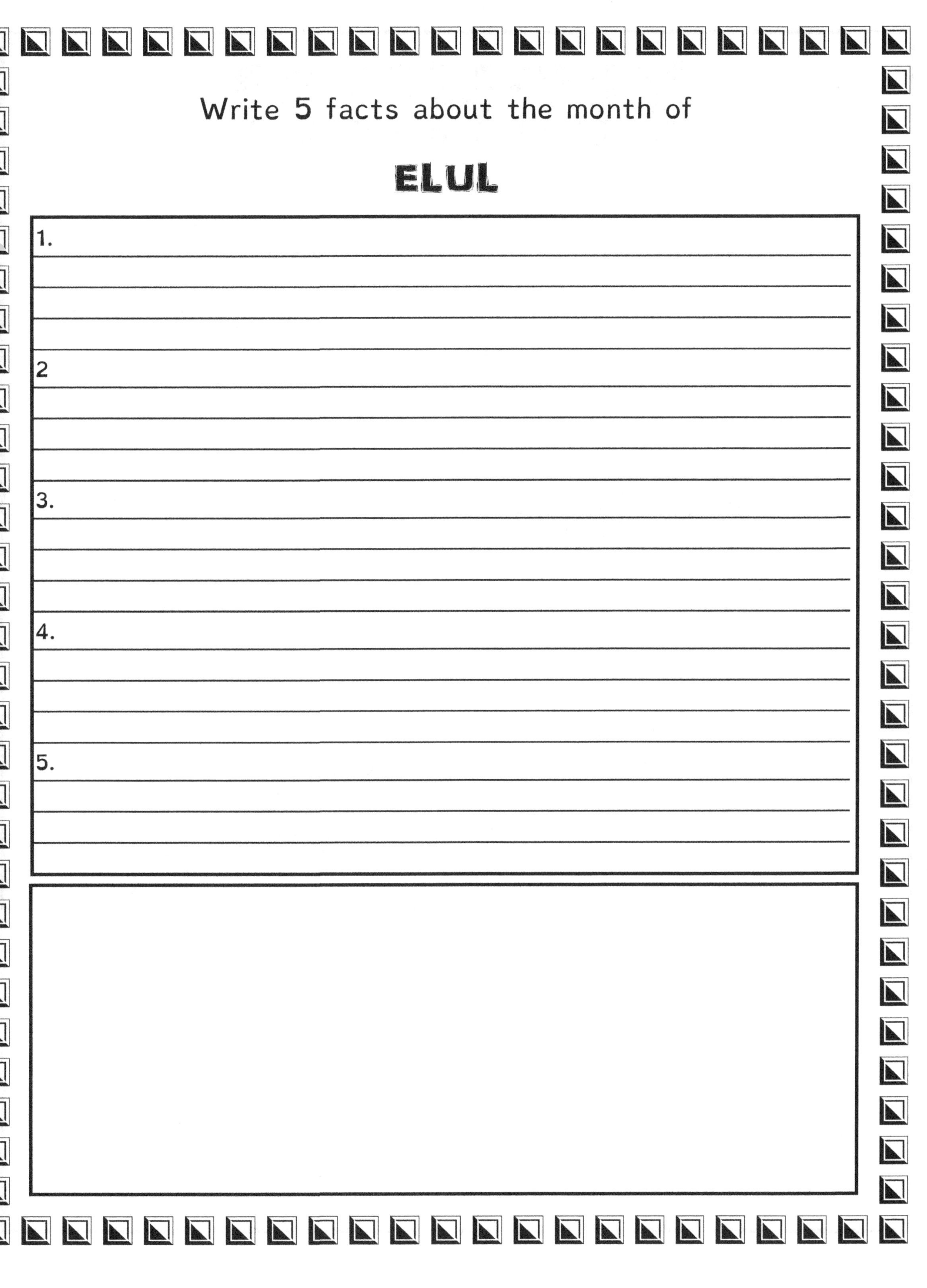

Write 5 facts about the month of
ELUL
1.
2
3.
4.
5.

TISHREI

Write 5 facts about the month of

TISHREI

1.

2

3.

4.

5.

Scriptures:

ROSH HASHANA

Gregorian Calendar Date:

Hebrew Calendar Date:

History:

Personal Thoughts, Prayers and Memories:

Planning:

Shopping List:

To Do List:

Customs & Traditions:

Recipe One:

Recipe Two:

Recipe Three:

Recipe Four:

ROSH HASHANA WORDSEARCH

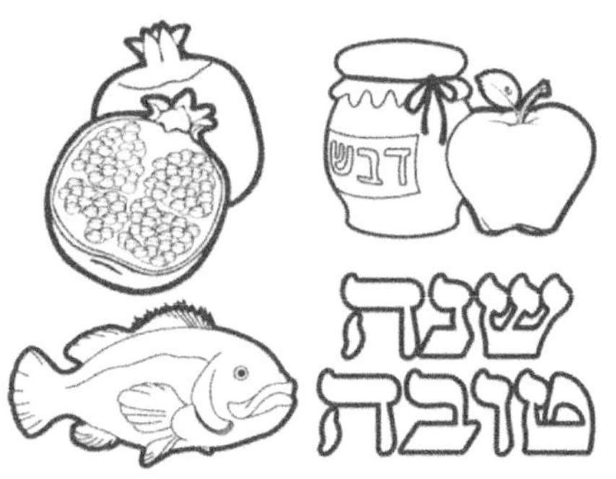

Find and circle the following words that are commonly associated with Rosh Hashana:

V	M	I	A	R	O	N	M	I	M	A	Y	L	O
C	O	L	S	H	A	N	A	T	O	V	A	H	F
M	T	I	A	L	M	A	H	Z	O	R	A	M	E
E	Z	T	A	I	H	T	O	O	T	H	V	C	H
C	O	T	V	M	E	A	K	G	O	A	K	I	C
Y	M	Y	O	M	T	S	H	A	H	V	H	I	A
O	K	S	E	S	H	L	E	H	C	U	V	A	E
M	A	S	H	L	G	I	H	A	I	H	V	H	M
T	L	A	L	O	H	C	E	K	L	S	M	Y	A
O	H	G	M	S	F	H	K	E	E	E	I	A	S
V	T	L	R	T	O	A	E	D	S	T	S	H	G
T	O	I	U	O	N	S	R	A	T	L	E	A	A
T	H	K	A	L	O	O	T	H	A	A	A	O	H
L	H	A	N	N	E	U	R	U	A	A	A	E	C

AKEDAH
TZOM KAL
YOM TOV
YAMIM NORAIM
ELUL
LSHANA TOVAH
TESHUVAH
SHOFAR
CHAG SAMEACH
HET
MAHZOR
SELICHOT
TASLICH

Play this puzzle online at : https://thewordsearch.com/puzzle/2175772/

Write down three facts about the shofar:

1.____

2.____

3.____

Draw or paste a picture of a shofar here

Write down three facts about The Days of Awe :

1.____

2.____

3.____

Draw or paste a picture depicting The Days of Awe here

TASHLICH

Write down 5 facts about Tashlich. Include facts about its history and significance:

1.

2.

3.

4.

5.

To read the Tashlich prayer, visit this link: www.myjewishlearning.com/article/text-of-tashlich/

"He will take us back in love; He will cover up our iniquities. You will hurl all our sins into the depths of the sea." (Micah 7:19)

Everybody makes mistakes. Thankfully, our mistakes do not have to define us and hold us captive. One of the beautiful things about the Tashlich ceremony is that it represents the washing away of past sins or mistakes. Write down mistakes you have made over this past year on the "slips of paper" below. Find a body of water like a river, stream, or pond (even a kiddie pool or bathtub filled with water will work!) and do Tashlich by casting your "sins" into the water. Small pebbles are convenient and do not harm the animals living in the water! Come back to this page and cover each "sin" with a piece of blue construction paper. How do you feel?

MY ROSH HASHANA GOALS/RESOLUTIONS

Rosh Hashana is the perfect time to create new goals and resolutions for the new year. Write down your goals or resolutions in the apples below. To ensure your success, make sure that your goals are SMART: specific, measurable, achievable, relevant and time-bound.

AKEIDA

(THE BINDING OF ISAAC)

The story of the binding of Isaac found in Genesis 22 is traditionally recited on Rosh Hoshana.

Read Genesis 22 and then create a comic to tell the story.

MY ROSH HASHANA

Draw pictures, paste photographs, and journal about your

SCRAPBOOK

favorite memories of your celebration on these pages.

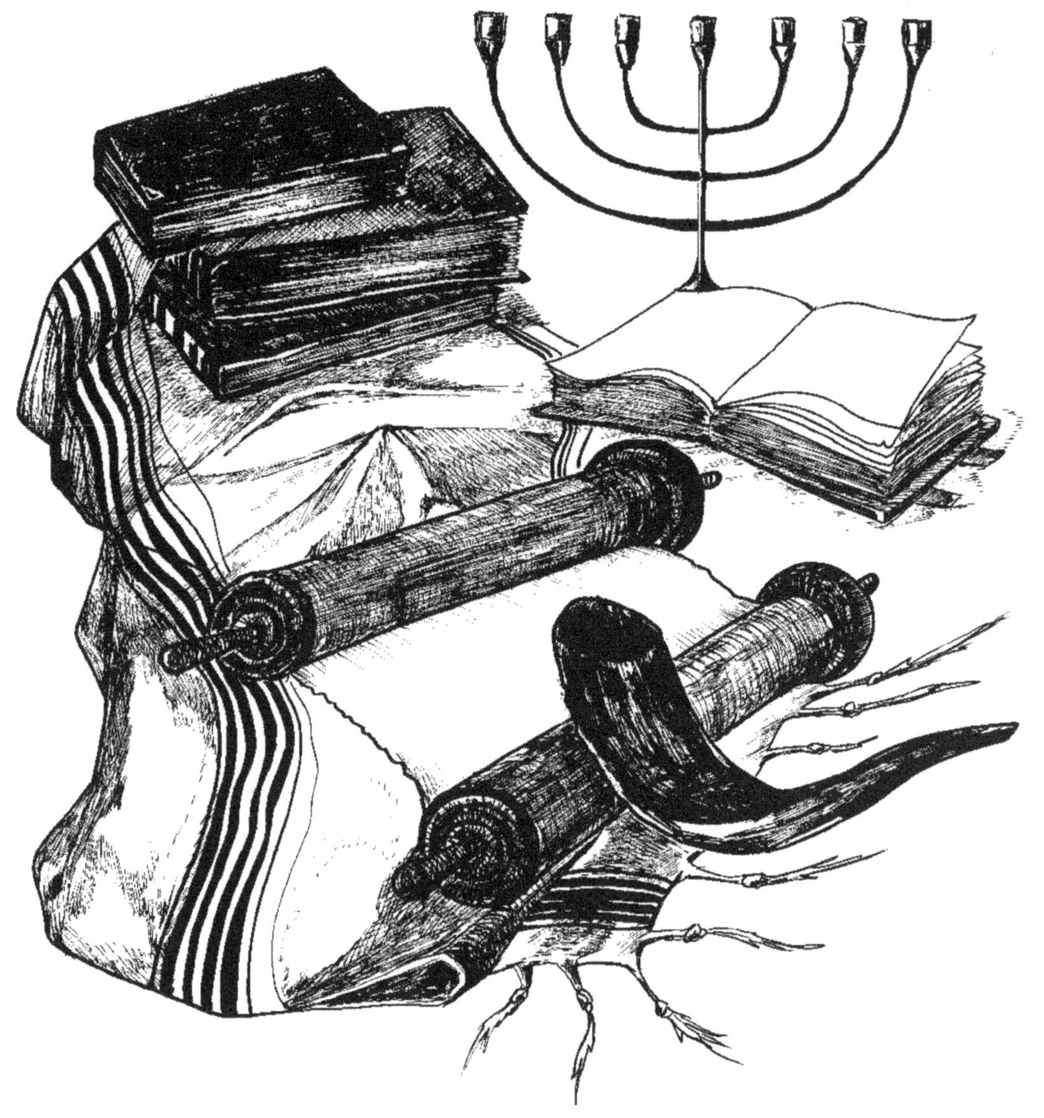

Scriptures:

YOM KIPPUR

Gregorian Calendar Date:

Hebrew Calendar Date:

History:

Personal Thoughts, Prayers and Memories:

Planning:

Shopping List:

To Do List:

Customs & Traditions:

Recipe One:

Recipe Two:

Recipe Three:

Recipe Four:

Sometimes the mistakes we make hurt other people. When this happens, it is important to apologize and seek forgiveness; make right the wrong. Write a letter to a person that you have hurt. Apologize for what you did and ask for forgiveness.

THE STORY OF JONAH

On Yom Kippur, it is traditional to read the story of Jonah. Write a modern day re-telling of this story below. Illustrate your story.

Scriptures:

SUKKOT

Gregorian Calendar Date:

Hebrew Calendar Date:

History:

Personal Thoughts, Prayers and Memories:

Planning:

Shopping List:

To Do List:

Customs & Traditions:

Recipe One:

Recipe Two:

Recipe Three:

Recipe Four:

BUILDING A SUKKAH

Design and build your own sukkah with your family! Remember these important criteria when building your sukkah:

- Must have 3 walls
- Must have a roof made of natural materials (i.e. tree branches, bamboo, wood, etc.) that allows the stars to be visible at night

Decorate your sukkah however you wish, though it is customary to use autumn or harvest materials. Spend us much time in your sukkah as possible and remember to invite your friends and neighbors!

Materials I will need:

Draw your sukkah decorations here

What I did in my sukkah:

Paste a photo of your completed sukkah here

Draw your sukkah design here:

THE FOUR SPECIES OF SUKKOT

"And you shall take for yourselves on the first day the fruit of a hadar (beautiful) tree, the branch of the palm trees, a bough from the "avot" tree, and willows of the stream, and you shall rejoice before your G-d for seven days."

Leviticus 23:40

Research the meaning and significance of the four species of Sukkot and record your findings below. On the following page, draw and label each of the four species.

MY SUKKOT

Draw pictures, paste photographs, and journal about your

SCRAPBOOK

favorite memories of your celebration on these pages.

Scriptures:

SHEMINI ATZERET & SIMCHAT TORAH

Gregorian Calendar Date:

Hebrew Calendar Date:

History:

Personal Thoughts, Prayers and Memories:

Recipe One:

Recipe Two:

Recipe Three:

Recipe Four:

PRAYER FOR RAIN

The "Prayer for Rain" is traditionally recited on Shemini Atzeret.

Read the translation and copy it on the lines provided:

Our G-d and G-d of our ancestors:
Remember Abraham who flowed to You like water.
You blessed him like a tree planted by streams of water.
You rescued him from fire and water.
He passed Your test by planting good deeds by every source of water.
For Abraham's sake, do not keep back water.
Remember Isaac, whose birth was foretold
when Abraham offered the angels a little water.
You asked his father to spill his blood like water.
In the desert Isaac dug and found wells of water.
For Isaac's sake, do not keep back water.
Remember Jacob, who crossed the Jordan's water.
He bravely rolled the stone off the mouth of the well of water.
He wrestled with an angel made of fire and water,

Remember Moses, who was drawn in a reed basket out of the Nile's water.

Who helped Jethro's daughters: He drew water and gave the sheep water.

He struck the rock and out came water.

For Moses' sake do not hold back water!

Remember Aaron, the High Priest, who, on Yom Kippur, washed himself five times with water,

He prayed and was sprinkled with purifying water,

He kept apart from a people who were as unstable as water.

For Aaron's sake do not hold back water.

Remember the Twelve Tribes whom

You brought through the divided waters;

For whom You sweetened bitter water;

Their descendants' blood was spilled like water.

Turn to us, G-d, who are surrounded by troubles like water.

Simchat Torah marks the ending of one Torah reading cycle and the beginning of the next. Look up this year's Torah reading schedule and begin reading each Parsha ("Portion") with your family every Shabbat. Below, copy your favorite verse/verses from the Torah and add an illustration:

(c) Ann D. Koffsky

CHESHVAN

Write 5 facts about the month of

CHESVAN

1.

2

3.

4.

5.

KISLEV

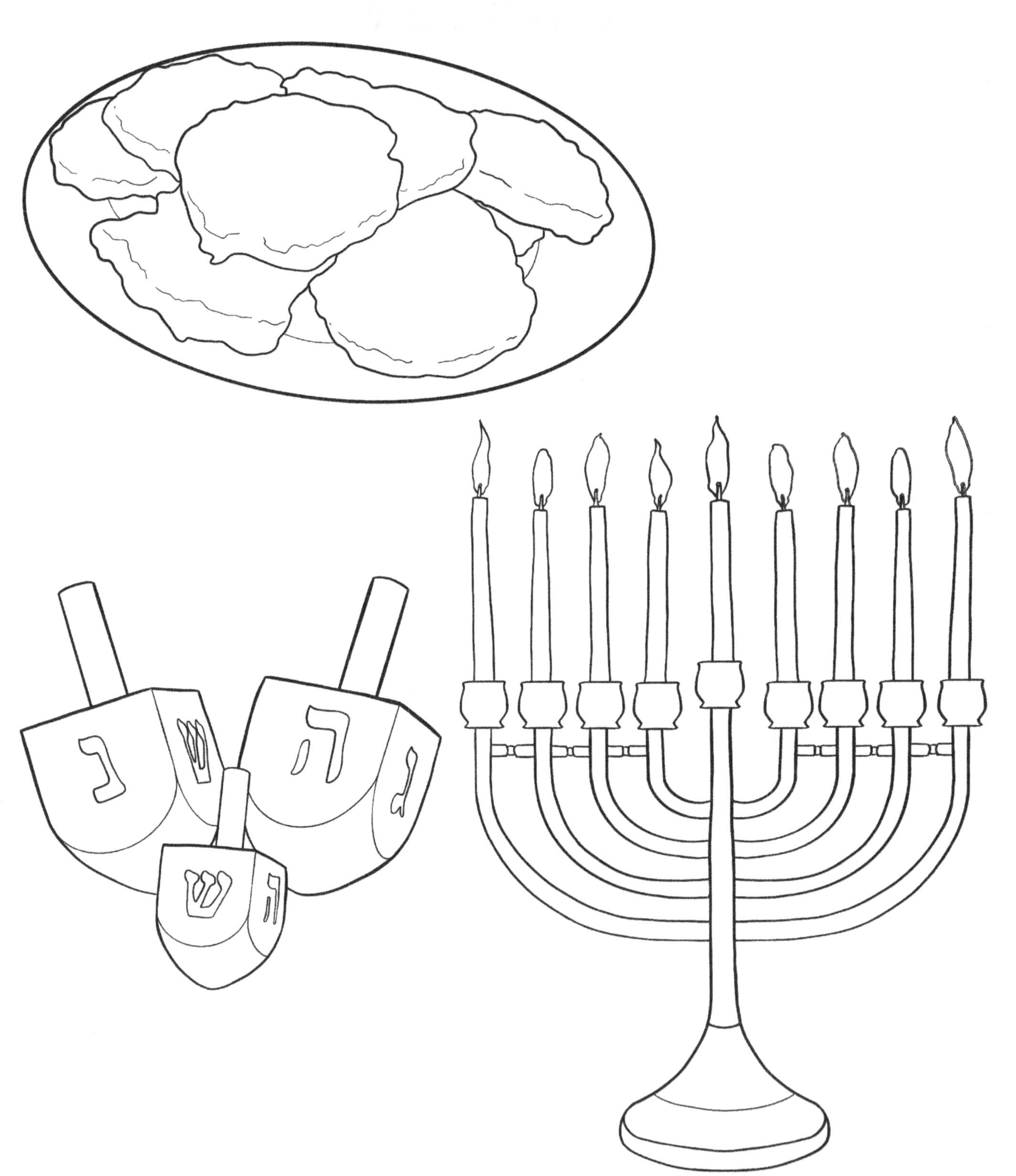

Write 5 facts about the month of

KISLEV

1.

2

3.

4.

5.

Scriptures:

CHANUKAH

Gregorian Calendar Date:

Hebrew Calendar Date:

History:

Personal Thoughts, Prayers and Memories:

Planning:

Shopping List:

To Do List:

Customs & Traditions:

Recipe One:

Recipe Two:

Recipe Three:

Recipe Four:

THE MACCABEAN REVOLT

Extra! Extra! Read all about it!

You are the reporter. Research the Maccabean revolt and record your notes in the space below. When you have finished taking your notes, write an article about this event on the newspaper template provided. Keep in mind the "5 Ws": Who, what, when, where, and why. Who was involved, what happened, when did it happen, where did it happen, and why did it happen. Don't forget to add a title and illustrations or photos.

The Thinking Tree Times

Issue: ____________________ Date: ____________________

DREIDEL, DREIDEL, DREIDEL!

How to play the Dreidel game:

1. Two or more players can play.

2. Each player begins the game with an equal number of gelt (chocolate coins). Other small items such as coins, nuts, chocolate chips, raisins, etc. can be used in place of gelt.

3. At the beginning of each round, each player puts one piece into the center pot. (*Whenever the pot is empty or has only one game piece left, each player should put another piece into the pot.)

4. Take turns spinning the dreidel. Whatever Hebrew letter is face up when the dreidel stops determines the course of action:

    - *Nun* **נ** means "nothing." Do not give or receive any tokens.
    - *Gimel* **ג** means "everything." Take all the tokens from the pot.
    - *Hey* **ה** means "half." Take half of the tokens in the pot.
    - *Shin* **ש** (or *Peh* **פ** if playing in Israel) means "put in." Put one token into the pot.

5. If a player runs out of tokens, that player is "out" or may ask another player for a "loan."

6. When one person has taken all the tokens, the game is over.

HISTORY OF THE DREIDEL

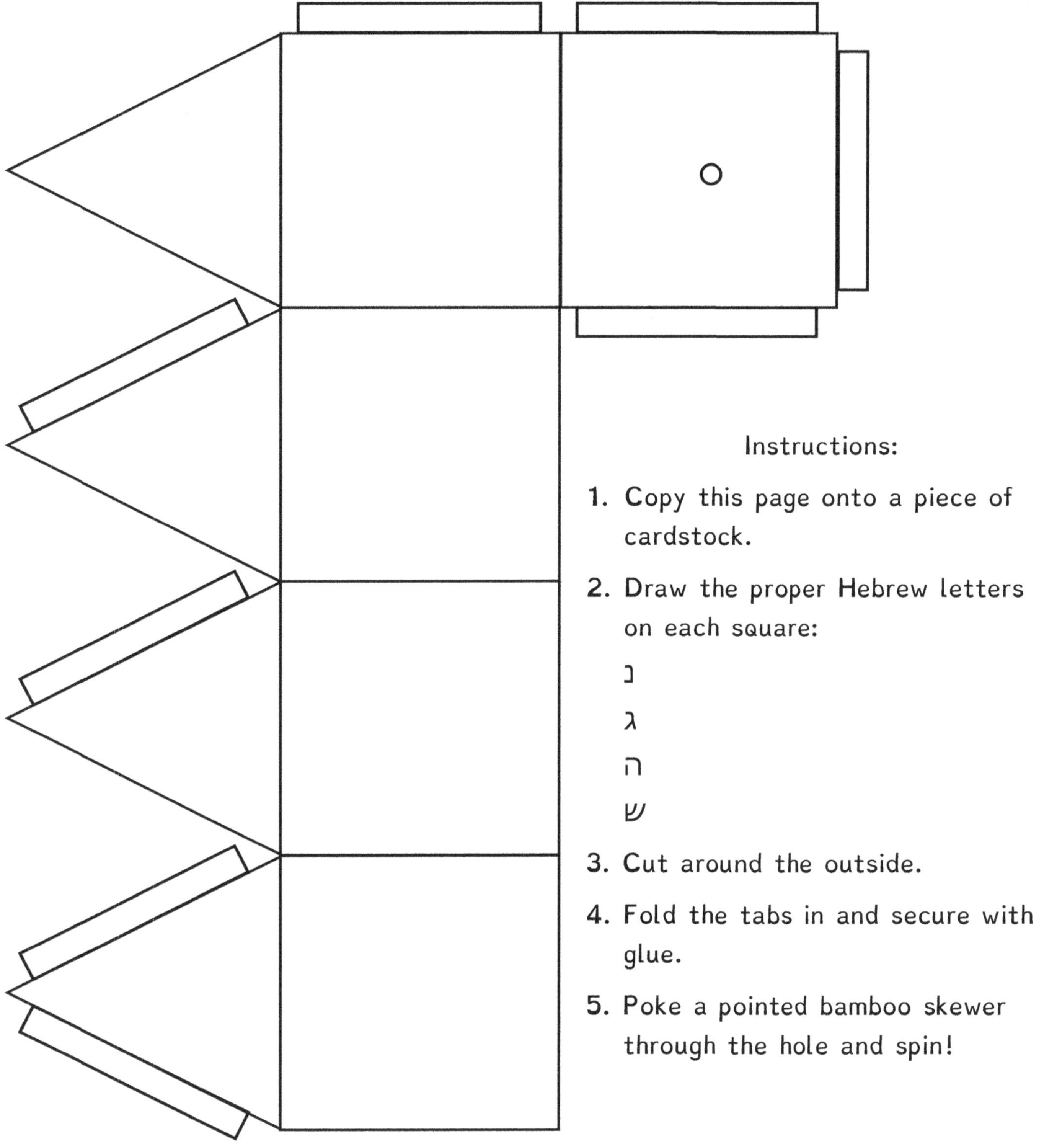

Instructions:

1. Copy this page onto a piece of cardstock.
2. Draw the proper Hebrew letters on each square:

   נ

   ג

   ה

   ש
3. Cut around the outside.
4. Fold the tabs in and secure with glue.
5. Poke a pointed bamboo skewer through the hole and spin!

The letters on the Dreidel stand for a saying. What is that saying?

____

____

____

MY CHANUKAH

Draw pictures, paste photographs, and journal about your

SCRAPBOOK

favorite memories of your celebration on these pages.

TEVET

Write 5 facts about the month of

TEVET

1.

2

3.

4.

5.

SHVAT

Write 5 facts about the month of

SHVAT

1.

2

3.

4.

5.

Scriptures:

TU B'SHEVAT

Gregorian Calendar Date:

Hebrew Calendar Date:

History:

Personal Thoughts, Prayers and Memories:

Planning:

Shopping List:

To Do List:

Customs & Traditions:

HAPPY BIRTHDAY, TREES!

Tu B'Shevat is a minor Jewish holiday that is traditionally celebrated by planting trees. It is also a day to celebrate nature and focus on being a good steward of your environment. If you can't plant a tree today because of the climate conditions in your area, consider planting parsley instead. Your parsley should be ready to be harvested in time for your Passover Seder! Follow the instructions below to start your parsley indoors. Look up the planting guidelines for your area to determine the best time to transplant your seedling outside.

What you will need to plant parsley indoors:

1. Parsley seeds (best to soak overnight before planting)
2. small container (empty yogurt container, small pot, etc)
3. potting soil
4. water

Plant your parsley!

1. Poke small holes in the bottom of your container for drainage. Parsley likes well draining soil.
2. Fill your container 3/4 full with potting soil.
3. Make a small indentation about 1/4 inch deep in the soil with your index finger.
4. Drop 3-4 parsley seeds into the hole. (TIP: soak your seeds overnight to improve your chances of success.)
5. Cover the seeds with soil.
6. Dampen the soil with a little bit of water (do not over water!).
7. Place your container in a sunny window.
8. Keep the soil moist but do not over water!
9. Parsley is slow to germinate. Seedlings might take 3-4 weeks to appear.
10. Your parsley is ready to harvest when the leaf stems have 3 segments. Cut leaves from the outer portion and leave the inner portion to mature.

MY TU B'SHEVAT "7 SPECIES" MEAL PLAN

Create a vegetarian meal plan that uses each of the 7 species found in Deuteronomy 8:8: wheat, barley, grapes, figs, pomegranates, olives, and dates. Use the following 2 pages to record your favorite recipes.

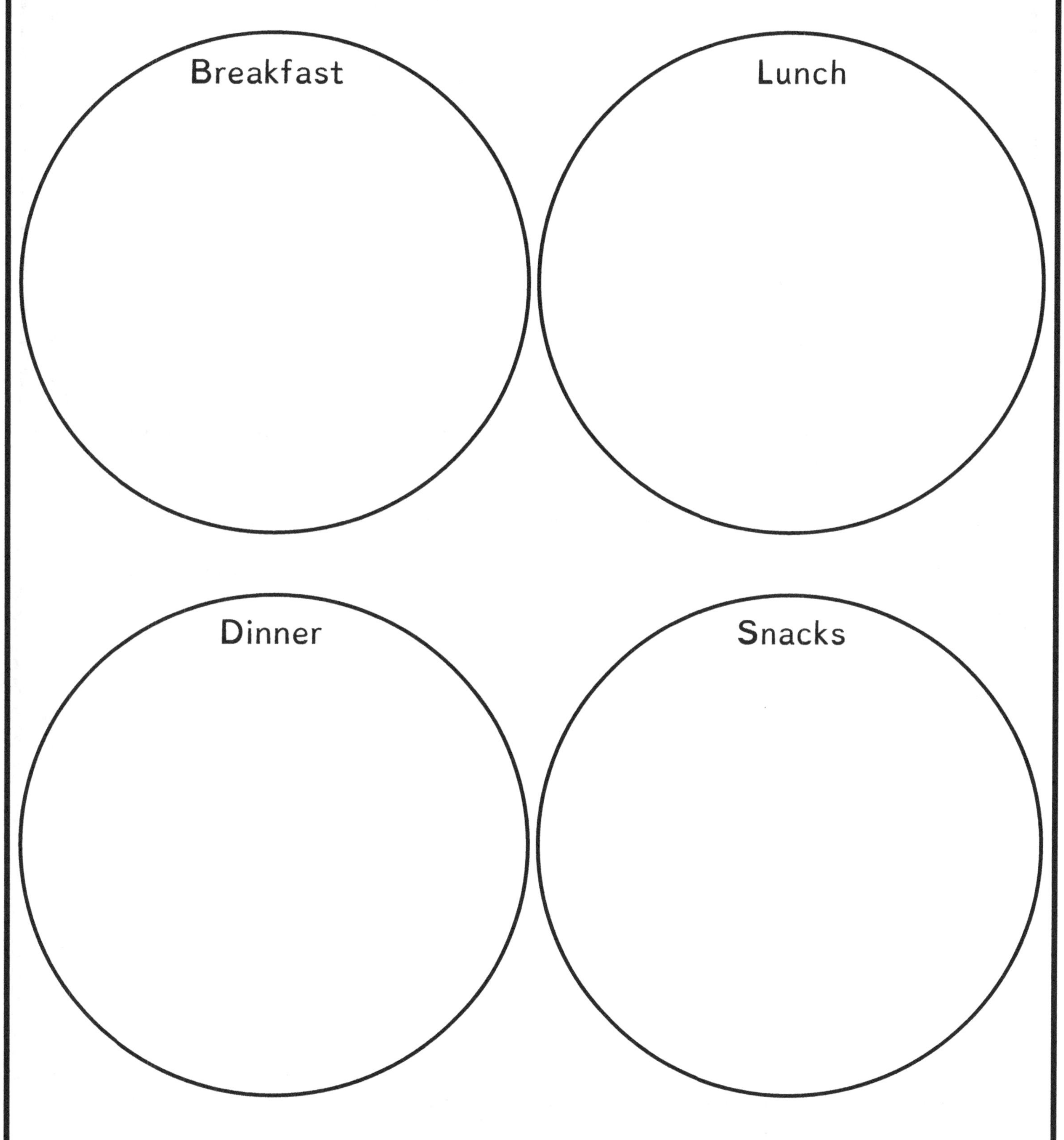

Recipe One:

Recipe Two:

Recipe Three:

Recipe Four:

ADAR

Write 5 facts about the month of

ADAR

1.

2

3.

4.

5.

Scriptures:

PURIM

Gregorian Calendar Date:

Hebrew Calendar Date:

History:

Personal Thoughts, Prayers and Memories:

Planning:

Shopping List:

To Do List:

Customs & Traditions:

Recipe One:

Recipe Two:

Recipe Three:

Recipe Four:

DESIGN YOUR OWN PURIM MASK

Purim is a time of celebration when many children enjoy dressing up in costumes. Be creative and design your own Purim mask below!

MY FAVORITE HAMANTASCHEN RECIPE

Ingredients:

Directions:

Draw a picture or paste a photo of your Hamantaschen here:

Prep Time:

Oven Temp:

Cook Time:

MY PURIM FEAST

Gather together your family, friends, and neighbors and have a Purim feast! Use the recipes you have collected and create your meal plan:

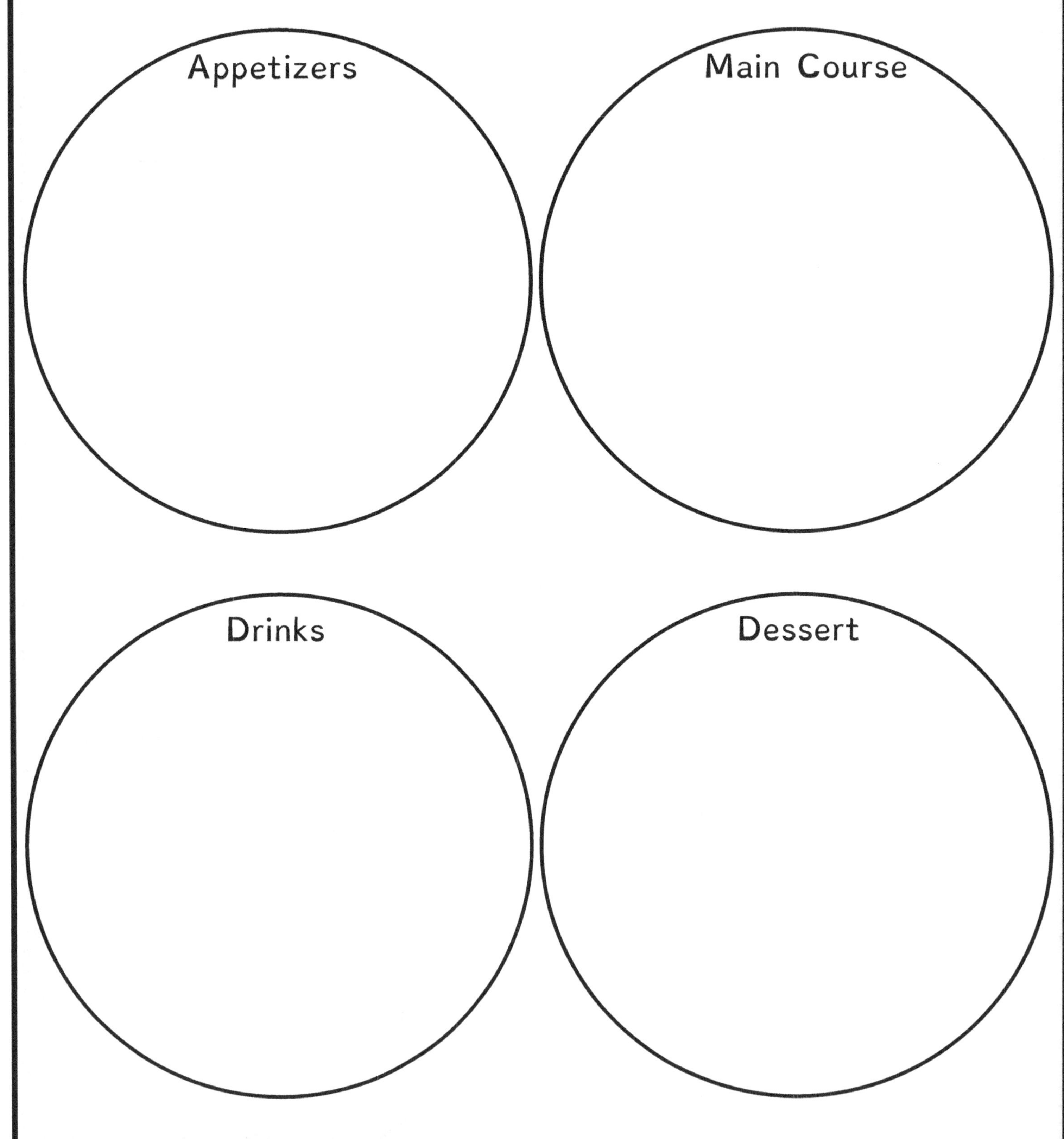

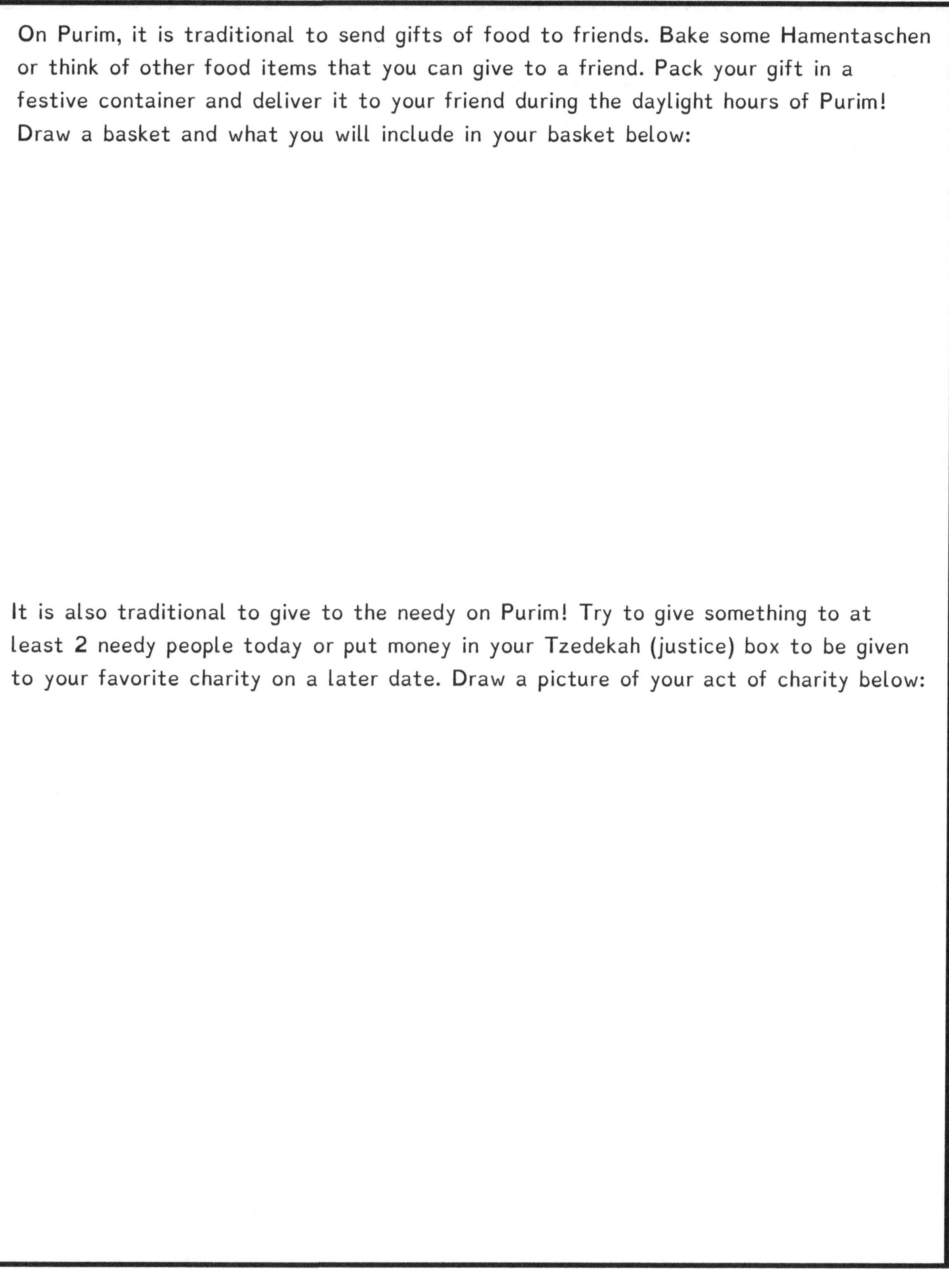

On Purim, it is traditional to send gifts of food to friends. Bake some Hamentaschen or think of other food items that you can give to a friend. Pack your gift in a festive container and deliver it to your friend during the daylight hours of Purim! Draw a basket and what you will include in your basket below:

It is also traditional to give to the needy on Purim! Try to give something to at least 2 needy people today or put money in your Tzedekah (justice) box to be given to your favorite charity on a later date. Draw a picture of your act of charity below:

Write an Acrostic poem about the story of Queen Esther using the first letters of her name. Illustrate your poem on the next page:

Q ______________________________

U ______________________________

E ______________________________

E ______________________________

N ______________________________

E ______________________________

S ______________________________

T ______________________________

H ______________________________

E ______________________________

R ______________________________

MY PURIM

Draw pictures, paste photographs, and journal about your

favorite memories of your celebration on these pages.

LIFECYCLE EVENTS

In addition to the many major and minor Jewish holidays, there are many life events called "lifecycle" events that are celebrated by Jewish people all over the world. These events include (but are not limited to): Brit Milah, naming ceremony, Upsherin, Bar/Bat Mitzvah, marriage, aging and retirement, death/mourning, etc. Each event has its own set of meaningful customs, traditions, and rituals. Do a little research on a few of the lifecycle events and record your findings on the following pages. You may photocopy the Customs and Traditions page for your own personal use if you wish to research more events.

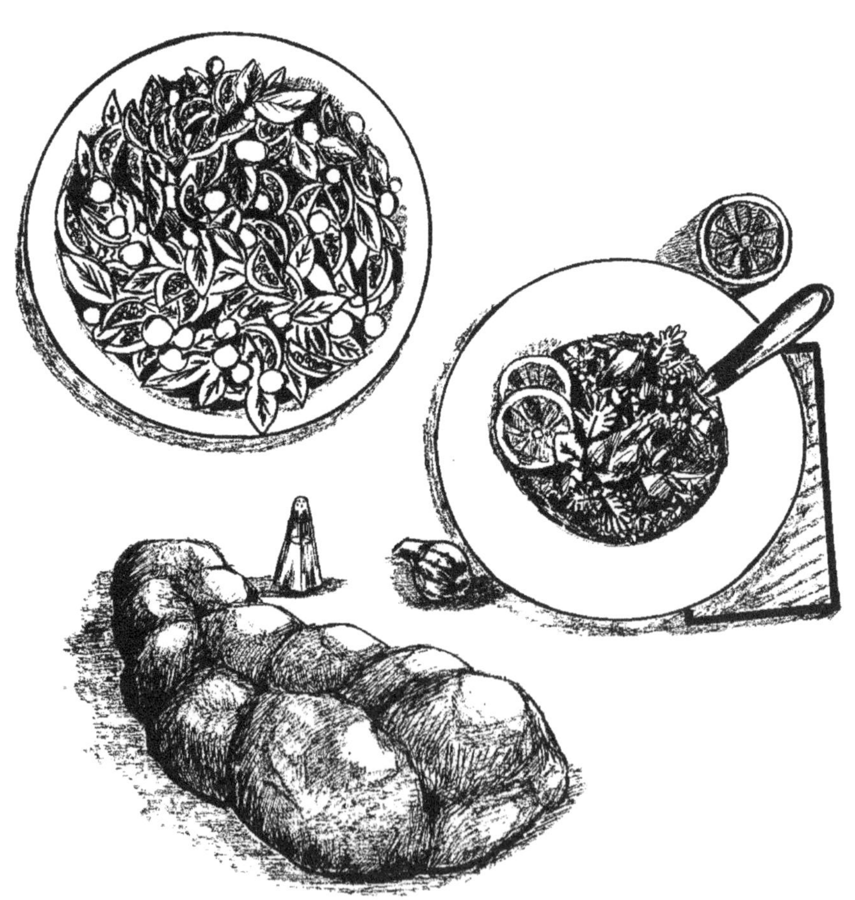

Customs & Traditions:

Customs & Traditions:

Customs & Traditions:

FUN-SCHOOLING WITH THINKING TREE BOOKS

Contact Us:

The Thinking Tree LLC

317.622.8852

FunSchoolingBooks.com DyslexiaGames.com

info@funschooling.com

The Dyslexie font is used in this book›

THE Thinking TREE
PUBLISHING COMPANY
ART
LOGIC
SCIENCE
SPELLING
READING
COLORING
THINKING
DRAWING
CREATING
Sarah Janisse Brown

Made in the USA
Las Vegas, NV
27 February 2025

18796913R00118